Seven Weeks to

Health and Healing

Volume 1

BARBARA A. WILLIAMS

Seven Weeks to Health & Healing (Volume 1)

Copyright © 2004 by Barbara A. Williams
All rights reserved.

Published by **Lighthouse Publishing Co.**
Detroit, Michigan
Cleveland, Ohio

ISBN: 978-0-9788675-3-9

Scripture taken from
Holy Bible, The King James Version
Copyright © 1976 by Thomas Nelson Publishers, Inc. Nashville, TN

Page and Cover Design, Shannon Crowley
Treasure Image & Publishing
TreasureImagePublishing.com

Rev. Barbara A. Williams
The Ministry of the Watchman International
P.O. Box 43334
Cleveland, Ohio 44143
1-800-560-9240
www.ministryofthewatchman.com

Dedication

This book is dedicated in loving memory of my late husband, Aubrey D. Williams, Jr., who loved these daily meditations.

*His encouragement and strength sustained me through the many years of our marriage,
and I thank God for the life we shared.*

Introduction

I wrote this book as a daily devotional to help believers focus on the Lord Jesus Christ. The daily readings are thought provoking while being brief and to the point. This format is one that fits easily into our modern lifestyles.

As believers we are admonished by God to "meditate on the word day and night..." God promises that if we will do this we will have prosperous ways and good success. I encourage the people of God in success. There is nothing I enjoy more than to see the people of God enjoying all the success that God has planned for them.

Daily meditation on God's word inspires and encourages us. It helps us focus on wholesome, good and pure thoughts. Meditation on the Word gives us God's view and vision for our lives. It gives us hope and rest in our souls. Meditation on God's word is the greatest mental health exercise we can employ. God's word heals, saves and delivers. I hope you enjoy meditating with God through the teaching in this book.

Contents

8	Week One
14	Week Two
20	Week Three
26	Week Four
32	Week Five
38	Week Six
44	Week Seven

You are More Healed <u>NOW</u> Than You Ever Have Been!

WEEK ONE

Healing Scripture to Meditate for the Week...

If you are in need of healing, there is good news! Proverbs 4:20-22 SAYS:

"My son, attend to my words; incline thine ear unto my sayings. Let them not depart from thine eyes; keep them in the midst of thine heart. For they are life unto those that find them, and health to all their flesh."

So there is life and health in God's word. Since God's word is medicine, we must take it like we would a prescription. I suggest three times a day, like you would your food. Remember, healing is the children's bread. Consider this your "dose" for today. Remember, read, and meditate three times a day the following:

Rx: <u>ACTS</u> <u>10:38</u> ~ How God anointed Jesus of Nazareth with the Holy Ghost and with power: who went about doing good, and healing all that were oppressed of the devil; for God was with Him.

DOING GOOD ALWAYS BRINGS HEALING

MONDAY

How God anointed Jesus of Nazareth with the Holy Ghost and with power: who went about doing good, and healing all that were oppressed of the devil; for God was with Him.
Acts 10:38

Jesus was anointed of God and went about doing good. The anointing causes us to do good. 1 John 2:20 tells us that we have an unction from the Holy One and we know all things. This inner anointing causes us to have the knowledge of God, for He knows all things. This knowledge only speaks of good things, for God is good. Relying on the inner unction helps us to be like Jesus, we go about doing good and healing all who are oppressed of the devil, because God is with Him by virtue of the anointing. This unction is God with us. This unction only causes us to do good and heal. Whenever we have the unction to do good, we bring healing into that situation.

TUESDAY

How God anointed Jesus of Nazareth with the Holy Ghost and with power: who went about doing good, and healing all that were oppressed of the devil; for God was with Him.
Acts 10:38

What does it mean to go about doing good? This means that you do good everywhere you go. "Gee, Barb, that's a tall order." For man to do this on his own is a tall order, but it is not for God. The unction, which is the very life of God, knows no partiality, for God is no respecter of persons. This means that as long as we obey the unction, we will be impartial, just like God is. The more we imitate Him, the more good we do. When we are like God, we do good. This is why God redeemed us. He desires to live in us and live His life through us. Jesus is the healer and healing is good. Everywhere He went, He did good. When people came to see Him, they expected good things. The expectation of goodness itself brought about healing. The people began to release their faith for the devil's oppression to leave, and Jesus was there to release the anointing to do good. Goodness brings healing.

Remember to thank God for healing you!

WEDNESDAY

How God anointed Jesus of Nazareth with the Holy Ghost and with power: who went about doing good, and healing all that were oppressed of the devil; for God was with Him.
Acts 10:38

The devil is the author of oppression. We see this many times in Jesus' healing ministry. People often blame illness on God, but it is clear from this scripture that God only does good. Is sickness good? No it is not. Sickness is listed in Deuteronomy 28 as part of the curse of the law. Poverty and death are the other aspects of the curse. Sickness was laid upon man as a penalty for the broken law. Whenever the law is broken, there must be a penalty paid for the act of disobedience. This penalty is carried out by Satan, for he was the first to break the law. Jesus says that Satan is the father of lies. A lie is the opposite of truth, which is good. The truth is, Jesus went about doing good and healing all. This was done so that God could fulfill the Messianic prophecy spoken by Isaiah, "Himself took our infirmities, and bear our sicknesses." Is healing good? Ask anyone who has been sick, especially for a long period of time. Ask people who are waiting for organ donations, chemotherapy or major surgery. Satan is the oppressor. Jesus' goodness removes his oppression.

Remember...
By Jesus' stripes
YOU ARE HEALED!

THURSDAY

How God anointed Jesus of Nazareth with the Holy Ghost and with power: who went about doing good, and healing all that were oppressed of the devil; for God was with Him.
Acts 10:38

Goodness is the essence of God. God anointed Jesus with the Holy Ghost and with power. The Holy Ghost and power is a good power. Many people are afraid of the power of God. Many do not understand the manifestations of the power of God, and with this lack of knowledge comes fear. When the power of God manifests, the person may experience warmth, shaking, stammering lips and may even fall under the power of God. Just because these manifestations may be new to the person, it does not mean that the power is not good. God's presence always brings a refreshing, and that is good. His power always removes sin, sickness, disease and oppression, which brings about healing. God's power to heal is different from natural power. Whenever we go to see the doctor, we can expect some pain or discomfort. Yet God heals without any pain at all. We may have reactions to and impressions about the power, but we are never hurt by it. He always does us good.

Remember...
Jesus Healed them ALL!

FRIDAY

How God anointed Jesus of Nazareth with the Holy Ghost and with power: who went about doing good, and healing all that were oppressed of the devil; for God was with Him.
Acts 10:38

The anointing to do good works in us, too. Have you ever thought about the fact that since you have been born again, you have more love, peace, joy and kindness than you have ever had in your life? Think about all the places you may go in the course of a day: home, work, super market, mall, cleaners, school, daycare, DMV, etc., etc. Consider that many people who visit these places do not abide in the fruit of the Spirit and cannot release these fruit wherever they go. If a clerk is slow to wait on you, the fruit of patience and kindness will sustain you through the wait if you will yield to them. Have you ever had a clerk remark how patient or kind you are? Have you ever noticed that they sometimes expect you to react negatively and you do not? This is a healing force that you bring into every situation of life. The expectation of bad has been replaced by good. This causes the clerk to take on a happier countenance, and a merry heart doeth good like a medicine. Joy has healing power. When we abide in the fruit of the Spirit and bring joy and happiness to others, we bring about healing to them.

Remember...
He has Loved YOU
with an Everlasting Love

WEEK TWO

Healing Scripture

to Meditate for the Week...

If you are in need of healing, there is good news! Proverbs 4:20-22 SAYS:

"My son, attend to my words; incline thine ear unto my sayings. Let them not depart from thine eyes; keep them in the midst of thine heart. For they are life unto those that find them, and health to all their flesh."

So there is life and health in God's word. Since God's word is medicine, we must take it like we would a prescription. I suggest three times a day, like you would your food. Remember, healing is the children's bread. Consider this your "dose" for today. Remember, read, and meditate three times a day the following:

Rx: <u>Matthew 8:17</u> ~ Himself took our infirmities, and bare our sicknesses.

HOW TO MAKE JESUS YOUR HEALER:
TRUST HIS WORD

MONDAY

And when Jesus was entered into Capernaum, there came unto Him a centurion, beseeching Him, And saying, Lord, my servant lieth at home sick of the palsy, grievously tormented. And Jesus saith unto him, I will come and heal him.
Matthew 8:5-7

Somebody needs Jesus. This is not news. Everybody will need Him one day. It is good to recognize our need for Him everyday, and cultivate a relationship with Him. But here is a man who is outside of the covenant of promise. Actually, this man is a pagan. His servant may be a pagan, also. He may be a Hebrew, but the nationality of the servant is not known. It is probably not important. This story lets us know that God's word is not a respecter of persons. Wherever the Word is believed and acted upon, Jesus will manifest Himself. He will cause to happen that which you request. He manifests Himself as Healer where we desire to be healed.

The person making the request here has compassion on his servant. There must be some element of love, care, and concern for the servant before a faith request can be made. That is why God judges us according to how much we love. Faith worketh by love. So here we have a man who is an idol worshipper requesting mercy for a servant who perhaps is not a worshipper of God either. What do you think their chances are for a healing? Well, that should give you hope, child of God, for you have a covenant of healing with Jesus, but you must initiate that covenant. You must make Him your healer.

TUESDAY

The centurion answered and said, Lord, I am not worthy that thou shouldest come under my roof: but speak the Word only, and my servant shall be healed.
For I am a man under authority, having soldiers under me: and I say to this man, Go, and he goeth; and to another, Come, and he cometh; and to my servant, Do this, and he doeth it.
Matthew 8:8-9

So Jesus has agreed to come and heal the servant. This man made Jesus his Healer through asking in faith. When Jesus agrees to come, the man is overwhelmed at His graciousness. Then he remembers something. Perhaps it is the condition of his house. Perhaps it is the carnality of his life represented by his manner of living. Perhaps he has carvings of Zeus and Juno. Perhaps there are dedicated things in his home. He knows that Jesus may be offended that he has not served Him, or that Jesus will know something about him that will make Him change His mind about healing his servant. He should not fear. Once Jesus gives His word about something, He will do it.

This man goes on to tell Jesus that he knows only His word of power is needed to heal the man. This is the highest form of faith. There are many people who brought the sick to Jesus, and there were many who were visited in their homes, as they were too sick to travel. Lazarus was one whom Jesus had to visit to heal. Jesus still makes house calls, and this centurion had the key to it. He knew that Jesus healed by His word only. His word was anointed with power, but the centurion had to get Jesus to speak the Word specifically to his servant. It is not enough to know that Jesus heals others. We must know that He heals us. This centurion knew this.

WEDNESDAY

When Jesus heard it, He marvelled, and said to them that followed, Verily I say unto you, I have not found so great faith, no, not in Israel.
Matthew 8:10

His understanding caused Jesus to marvel. Jesus then compares this pagan to Israel, His own. He came unto His own, but His own received Him not. Jesus comes to us many times offering help, and we refuse it. Have you ever been in a service where an altar call is made, and you know you should go up, but you're "not sure"? Perhaps you felt moved to write to a ministry or sign up for mailings, or publications, but you didn't because you didn't want another piece of mail to come to your house. This is Jesus offering help, but we must first obey in order to get it. This is why He marveled at the centurion's faith. He saw that this man had gone beyond a mere superficial understanding of Him. This man had spent time studying the works of Jesus and had decided that Jesus will heal all who come by faith, and that He uses His authority over disease to do it. How did Jesus do this? Well, Himself took our sicknesses and bare our infirmities. He took them already. Whatever He has taken, He has possession of and authority over. He took it from us, so that we could be healed by His Word. He has given His word to all believers that He has paid for our healing...He has certainly taken it by the stripes of His body. We are healed.

THURSDAY

And I say unto you, That many shall come from the east and west, and shall sit down with Abraham, and Isaac, and Jacob, in the kingdom of heaven. But the children of the kingdom shall be cast out into outer darkness: there shall be weeping and gnashing of teeth.
Matthew 8:11-12

Jesus teaches the people that there is a reward for faith and a penalty for unbelief. If the centurion can have faith, then anybody can. He rebukes the children of Israel for their unbelief and lets them know that there is accountability for using or not using our faith to trust God. The people who are cast into outer darkness will be frustrated enough to gnash their teeth in anger at themselves for not believing Jesus, even though He proved His ministry with signs and wonders. This teaching also opens the kingdom to whosoever believes. Until this time the children of Israel felt that they had a "corner" on the knowledge of the Kingdom, but now they see Jesus accepting and commending a pagan Roman. God honors faith in Him and He is no respecter of persons. Jesus demonstrates that faith has no color, nationality or race. Faith is the Spirit of God, and God pours out His Spirit on all flesh.

Remember...
He will Never Leave you nor forsake you!

FRIDAY

And Jesus said unto the centurion, Go thy way; and as thou hast believed, so be it done unto thee. And his servant was healed in the selfsame hour.
Matthew 8:13

So Jesus confirms His word with signs following. This is the reward of using our faith to believe God and take Him at His word. This centurion has now partaken of God's covenant. He has believed and trusted solely in God's word. He knows how the Kingdom works and has made Jesus his Healer. He has reached into a revelation that is necessary for us today. We must understand that the Word of God has healing power in it. We must believe that the Word of God is life and medicine to our flesh and if we receive it by hearing and believing, we can make Jesus our healer. We can be healed over and over again, because the Word never fails, and all the Words of God are full of power. We can trust Jesus as our healer by trusting and taking Him at His word.

Remember...
Give the Word Your
Full Attention

WEEK THREE

Healing Scripture to Meditate for the Week...

If you are in need of healing, there is good news! Proverbs 4:20-22 SAYS:

"My son, attend to my words; incline thine ear unto my sayings. Let them not depart from thine eyes; keep them in the midst of thine heart. For they are life unto those that find them, and health to all their flesh."

So there is life and health in God's word. Since God's word is medicine, we must take it like we would a prescription. I suggest three times a day, like you would your food. Remember, healing is the children's bread. Consider this your "dose" for today. Remember, read, and meditate three times a day the following:

Rx: <u>Exodus 23:25-26</u> ~ And ye shall serve the Lord your God, and He shall bless thy bread, and thy water; and I will take sickness away from the midst of thee. There shall nothing cast their young, nor be barren, in thy land: the number of thy days I will fulfil.

ATTEND TO YOUR HEALING UNTIL YOU GET IT

MONDAY

And straightway many were gathered together, insomuch that there was no room to receive them, no, not so much as about the door: and He preached the Word unto them.
Mark 2:2

Many people need to be healed. Some are trusting God for their healing, some are trusting natural means, some are not sure what they are trusting. They want to believe God, but they don't know where to start. The possibility of getting up and walking after being paralyzed for so long seems very remote. Yet somehow, here they all are at a Jesus meeting. There are many people here. Some need to be healed of various diseases and ailments, some like to witness miracles, some people just like to be in church every Sunday. Some are worshippers, some are religious, some are there to ask questions to see if they can trip up Jesus and accuse Him of some heresy. There are all kinds of people in attendance at a Jesus meeting. This is the press, (or crowd), that is preventing this man from getting to Jesus. The press can cause us to be distracted from our focus on receiving our healing. Proverbs 4:20 tells us we are healed by giving attention to the Word. Focusing our full attention on the Word causes it to become medicine to our flesh. Even though the crowd is pressing against Him, Jesus preaches anyhow. He continues to reach out to us with His Word. He wants to encourage our faith. He wants to make it easy for us to receive our healing.

TUESDAY

And they come unto Him, bringing one sick of the palsy, which was borne of four. And when they could not come nigh unto Him for the press, they uncovered the roof where He was: and when they had broken it up, they let down the bed wherein the sick of the palsy lay.
Mark 2:3-4

So these men are blocked from entering through the door to get their friend healed. We've all been there. We go to a large meeting and assume we will be healed there. We are reaching out the best way we know how. We try to keep our attention on the Word, but we're distracted. We are not as worshipful as we should be. We become distracted by someone we've run into whom we haven't seen in a long time; they begin to talk to us about the people we both know and how they are doing now. We say to ourselves that we would like to be healed today, but what we have isn't really a sickness, it's just an inconvenience. We pass up the opportunity to receive our healing today because we have been distracted. But the men in this story were not distracted. They decide that if they cannot get to Jesus one way, they will do it another. There is always another opportunity to receive what you need from God. How many people walk away from the healing service discouraged and dejected? Many give up because they didn't receive the first time they reached out. Each time you hear the Word, your faith is being built.

 Remember to thank God for healing you!

WEDNESDAY

When Jesus saw their faith, He said unto the sick of the palsy, Son, thy sins be forgiven thee.
Mark 2:5

Has Jesus seen your faith? How do we show Him our faith? We show it in the same way this man did. We refuse to quit pursuing Him. We keep listening to the Word. We keep going to Healing School. We continue to thank Jesus for healing us by the stripes that He received when He was crucified. We refuse to give up and say that this is only a minor thing. We refuse to put off pursuing Him until it is too late. When Jesus mentions our sins, are we quick to repent? Is it important to your healing that your sins be forgiven? Of course it is. Many times we don't pursue Jesus and receive our healing because we are afraid that our sins will be uncovered. But Jesus always forgives. This is the wonderful thing about Jesus the Healer. He is also the one who bore our sins. When we go to Him to be healed, He gives us forgiveness, too. We should never be afraid to approach Him for our needs. Our faith saves us, not our good works. If you believe that Jesus bore all of this for us, then you will not hesitate to get as close as you can to Him for any need that you have. Forgiveness of sins sometimes must precede healing.

Remember...
By Jesus' stripes
YOU ARE HEALED!

THURSDAY

But there were certain of the scribes sitting there, and reasoning in their hearts, Why doth this man thus speak blasphemies? who can forgive sins but God only? And immediately when Jesus perceived in his spirit that they so reasoned within themselves, He said unto them, Why reason ye these things in your hearts? Whether is it easier to say to the sick of the palsy, Thy sins be forgiven thee; or to say, Arise, and take up thy bed, and walk? But that ye may know that the Son of man hath power on earth to forgive sins, (He saith to the sick of the palsy,)
Mark 2:6-10

The press is beginning to complain on the inside. Some of the onlookers are disturbed at the preacher's doctrine. Many people who come to the healing service come to disagree with the minister; they are "reasoners" instead of receivers. Much of the preaching done in a service is done to correct wrong thinking on the part of the press. Preaching and teaching bring revelation, revealing the thoughts and intents of our hearts. Jesus is giving everybody at the service a chance to increase their faith. He tells these reasoners that He ministered to the sick man the way He did in order to teach the onlookers something. Sometimes we forget that there are many people in need in a healing service. Many need enlightenment and to have their doctrine straightened out before they become sick. Jesus is preparing them for success in the future if they will only believe His words. Many times the preacher ministers the way He does to convince people that the power is of God, not man. Why would Smith Wigglesworth kick a deformed baby to get it healed? Why was Jack Coe so rough in handling people sometimes? We never know the thoughts of the people who are looking on.

FRIDAY

I say unto thee, Arise, and take up thy bed, and go thy way into thine house. And immediately he arose, took up the bed, and went forth before them all; insomuch that they were all amazed, and glorified God, saying, We never saw it on this fashion.
Mark 2:11-12

Jesus gives the command that finishes the healing in this young man. There is a command of the Spirit of God that will complete our healing if we will stay focused on our healing until we get it. If we are not distracted on our first attempt to receive our healing, and continue to pursue Jesus the Healer, then we will get His attention. We must daily show Him our faith in Him as our Healer. We must be quick to repent and to forgive. We must know that He will keep His Word. Daily pursuit of Jesus the Healer will ensure that we eat our daily bread dose of healing, and cause Him to focus fully upon us to complete our healing. When He gives the command to be healed, be quick to respond to Him. If He tells you He will meet you at a certain meeting, make sure you attend that meeting. Time spent hearing the Word is never wasted. God is where the healing is; don't compel the healing to come to you. Pursue Him, stay focused, and don't give up!

Remember...
Jesus Healed them ALL!

WEEK FOUR

Healing Scripture to Meditate for the Week...

If you are in need of healing, there is good news!
Proverbs 4:20-22 SAYS:

"My son, attend to my words; incline thine ear unto my sayings. Let them not depart from thine eyes; keep them in the midst of thine heart. For they are life unto those that find them, and health to all their flesh."

So there is life and health in God's word. Since God's word is medicine, we must take it like we would a prescription. I suggest three times a day, like you would your food. Remember, healing is the children's bread. Consider this your "dose" for today. Remember, read, and meditate three times a day the following:

Rx: **Psalm 107:20** ~ He sent His Word, and healed them, and delivered them from their destructions.

HE SENT HIS WORD AND HEALED THEM

MONDAY

Then they cry unto the Lord in their trouble, and He saveth them out of their distresses.
Psalm 107:19

What happens when we cry unto the Lord? I know many of us mature, faith-filled believers cannot relate to such a condition, but the writer of this psalm knew exactly how a human being feels when he is distressed. He also knows the remedy. There is an activity that man can perform that releases the compassion of God. It is crying out to Him. When you are in distress you are not concerned about sounding holy or making the right confession of faith. When distress hits, you want relief. You may not ask the right way, or be biblically correct in your approach, but somehow you reach God. The children of Israel sighed under the weight of Egyptian bondage, and God heard them and raised up a deliverer. Rosa Parks refused to give up her seat to a white man, and God raised up a deliverer. We are still reaping the benefits of the civil rights acts, whether we are black, female, Hispanic, or any other minority. We have been delivered by the response of heaven to our affliction. God sends a Word and releases a power on earth that eventually remedies the problem. God moves by the power of His Word. He upholds the world by the Word of His power, and will not allow His holy ones to see corruption. We need only to cry out to Him and we find that He is mighty to deliver. He heals bodies, situations, nations, oppressed people, and all things by His Word.

TUESDAY

He sent His Word, and healed them, and delivered them from their destructions. Psalm 107:20

So God sends His Word and heals us. Has anybody given a healing Word to you? It is amazing how many hurting words we receive. If words cause pain, then they can cause healing. What we need is a Word with a healing balm on it. We need the Word that is higher than the hurtful words. We need the Word that is forever settled in heaven. We need a Word sent straight from God.

I can remember being a part of a local church where the members were very competitive. Certain people seemed to be involved in every area of ministry in the church or assumed authority in these areas. I was involved in a women's ministry outside the church, but for some reason the pastor often asked if I would use my gifts in the church. While I wanted to be helpful, I really didn't feel comfortable working there. There seemed to be too much open strife and confrontation among the leaders. Many times I was given things to do by the pastor only to see my work maligned by the others or given back to me as unusable. While I tried to be good-natured about it, the truth is, I was hurt by the lack of appreciation of my efforts. I know many people feel this way off and on, but not many people have worked for days on hand drawn posters and seen them on the floor of the storage room months later, never having been used by people who asked you to do them. I remember feeling quite discouraged one particular Sunday, and I was sitting on a bench near the exit door of the church. A little girl came up to me out of nowhere, kissed me on the cheek and said, "I love you, pretty lady." Well, that was a healing Word sent from heaven. I never knew who she was and couldn't remember what she looked like, but her words broke my mood of self-pity. I continued to be obedient to the pastor, even though his associates tried to make it hard for me. I began to trust God as my Healer. To this day, I have no fear of serving man. I live to please and obey God.

WEDNESDAY

*He sent His Word, and healed them, and delivered
them from their destructions.
Psalm 107:20*

When you need physical healing, God sends His Word and heals you. Keep crying out to Him. Cry out in faith, cry out with thanksgiving, and in the spirit of worship, trust, and adoration. When you connect to God, He always touches your need. In the book of Matthew, chapter 8, we see an example of a person who connected with Jesus, the Living Word of God. Jesus was sent to heal, because He himself took our infirmities and bore our sorrows.

Peter's mother was in bed sick with a fever. Pretty soon, Jesus appeared, touched her hand, and the fever left her. Perhaps she had cried out to God, or perhaps this was just the way Jesus operated. He felt obligated to take care of the disciples' families as well as the disciples. At any rate, this woman, who was in covenant with God, received healing because the Living Word of God was sent to her, and she was delivered from the fever that was trying to destroy her. She got out of bed and ministered to the men. She was restored to her normal way of living. This is another effect of God's Word: it restores what was stolen.

Remember...
He has Loved YOU
with an Everlasting Love

THURSDAY

He sent His Word, and healed them, and delivered them from their destructions.
Psalm 107:20

In Matthew 10:28-31, Jesus heals the blind who come to Him. In this instance, the Word, (already having been sent) must be received by the person in need in order for the healing to manifest. How do you receive the Word of God? Well, you have to refuse to reject it. Why? Because the carnal mind has a tendency to reject things that sound unfamiliar. That is why the gospel must be preached over and over again to the same people. Why does the Word of God sound unfamiliar? It sounds unfamiliar when we are bombarded with symptoms, when we feel sick, or when we have been handed a diagnosis of sickness. The symptoms, feelings, and sickness all bombard our minds with their false evidence. When we hear the Word, then faith comes with evidence of a cure and healing. When we confess the Word, we minister health and spiritual medicine to our bodies, and we begin to agree with the Word of healing. We become like the blind men. Jesus asked what they believed. They believed in Jesus' ability to heal them, which opened the door for them to receive their healing.

Remember…
He will Never Leave you nor forsake you!

FRIDAY

*He sent His Word, and healed them, and delivered
them from their destructions.*
Psalm 107:20

Then there is the woman with the issue of blood. She made her way through the crowd and pulled virtue out of Jesus and was healed. How was this so? God sent His Word, and she refused to let the Word pass her by without receiving it. This woman had spent all she had on doctors and was only worse, not better. Incurable, except for God. Does God care if He is our first resort or last resort? Apparently not. This woman began to rehearse in her mind what God was going to do for her. Is this possible? Of course it is. This is how we obtain. We begin to speak inside ourselves what we expect to happen. Sometimes we are disappointed. Some things that we think of often never come to pass. That is because they were fantasy; never conceived by God's Word. God's Word conceives truth... that which lasts. Whenever we have our hope in His Word, we will receive what we ask for if we don't give up. This woman was determined to get healed. Perhaps her faith kept her going to the doctors. At any rate, she was not defeated by their lack of ability to heal her. Instead she put her faith and expectancy in God this time. She heard about Jesus and set out to touch Him, for she knew that if she could touch Him she would be well. How did she know this? Her faith told her so. God sent His Word, which she believed, and she was made whole. Believe His Word will heal you. There is life, health and medicine in God's Word. Be healed in Jesus' name.

WEEK FIVE

Healing Scripture to Meditate for the Week...

If you are in need of healing, there is good news! Proverbs 4:20-22 SAYS:

"My son, attend to my words; incline thine ear unto my sayings. Let them not depart from thine eyes; keep them in the midst of thine heart. For they are life unto those that find them, and health to all their flesh."

So there is life and health in God's word. Since God's word is medicine, we must take it like we would a prescription. I suggest three times a day, like you would your food. Remember, healing is the children's bread. Consider this your "dose" for today. Remember, read, and meditate three times a day the following:

Rx: <u>Isaiah 53:5</u> ~ But He was wounded for our transgressions, He was bruised for our iniquities: the chastisement of our peace was upon Him; and with His stripes we are healed.

GOD'S MEDICINE, HIS WORD

MONDAY

My son, attend to my words; incline thine ear unto my sayings. Let them not depart from thine eyes; keep them in the midst of thine heart.
Proverbs 4:20-21

Instructions from God. Please pay attention. Whenever God gives instructions, we need to take heed to what He is saying and obey Him. If we are willing and obedient we will eat the good of the land. Many may be willing, but God does not honor our will; He honors our obedience. If we don't obey God, we will obey whatever pleases our flesh momentarily. Whatever we sow to the flesh will produce corruption. Disease and sickness are a type of corruption. In order to stop the process of corruption on our flesh, God intervenes and gives us instructions for our prosperity.

His instructions to prosper are consistent throughout His word. Isn't it wonderful that God never changes? He honors His word. His word is Him; it contains the very essence of God in all His glory. No wonder the Word must be given our full attention. The word is God. When we incline our ears to hear the Word, we are hearing God speak to us. When we keep the Word before our eyes we are beholding God; when we hide the Word in the midst of our hearts, we are inviting God inside.

It is impossible to separate God from His word. They are one. So if we want to keep God close, keep His word close. The Spirit will follow the Word. Focus on the Word, and the Spirit of God will cooperate with the Word. The Spirit of God then performs what the Word of God decrees. Keep the Word close by paying close attention to it.

TUESDAY

For they are life unto those that find them, and health to all their flesh.
Proverbs 4:22

The word is life to you if you find it. How do you find the Word? You find it through revelation. When you meditate on God's word, seek for it, keep it before your eyes, fight to hold it in your heart and not let it go in exchange for some thoughts that appeal to your carnal senses, you find the Word, and God begins to speak to you the deeper meaning of what you just meditated upon. Finding the Word also means finding the right promise that answers whatever need you might have. This is a marvelous thing that occurs when we keep the Word before us and hide it in our hearts. The word then begins to transform us and this transformation brings us from death and corruption into life. His life. Eternal life. The word of God has His eternal life in it. When we hide the Word in our hearts, we hide His life in our hearts.

There is yet another benefit of finding God's word and holding on to it in our hearts. It also brings health to all our flesh. This means that no matter what illness attacks your body or how many of them attack you at one time, inclining your ear to, holding on to and meditating upon His word, will bring health to your flesh. Many people can believe the Word heals the soul, but not the flesh. This scripture says that the Word is actually medicine to our flesh. Take the Word like medicine. Take as many doses per day as you like; it is impossible to take too much of the Word. When you are healed, if you continue to take it, you will stay healed and walk in Divine health. You then have an overflow of healing medicine in you. You can pray for others and they will be healed, too. What marvelous power there is in God's word.

WEDNESDAY

Keep thy heart with all diligence; for out of it are the issues of life. Put away from thee a froward mouth, and perverse lips put far from thee.
Proverbs 4:23-24

This is the prescription for keeping health. You must keep your heart. Why? Since the heart is the center of life, (all blood flows from the heart, which cleanses it, and returns it to all parts of the body) the Word says out of the heart comes the issues, or forces of life. The power of life flows from the heart. The heart feeds the thoughts and words spring from thoughts. The body is interconnected. All disease, then, is basically heart disease. Whatever is in your heart feeds your flesh, just as the blood flowing from the heart organ feeds every living cell in every part of the natural body. Whatever you hear eventually has an effect upon your heart. Whatever words you meditate upon eventually become deposited in your heart.

If we keep only the Word of God in our hearts, and guard with diligence the entrance into our hearts, we will have only life forces flowing out of our hearts. If we allow carnal, froward or perverse, deceitful or wicked words to proceed out of our mouths, then we are inclining our ears to corrupt words. The choice is ours. We may not be able to prevent hearing certain words, but we may certainly prevent keeping them in our hearts and allowing them to issue forth out of us.

Remember...
Give the Word Your
Full Attention

THURSDAY

Let thine eyes look right on, and let thine eyelids look straight before thee.
Proverbs 4:25

Keeping our eyes straight ahead means that we are willing to do things God's way. God leads us in a plain path. His word gives us a clear-cut vision into the future. There are no short cuts or detours on God's road. There is nothing for God to hide from us. There are no surprises. God is open, honest, pure and without guile. His word is a lamp and a light to our feet. There is no darkness or stumbling in Him. So the straight and plain path unfolds God's will before us. He is ever before us, leading us and guiding us. We must not look back. Remember Lot's wife. When we keep our eyes straight before us, we become available to be attentive to God. We wait for His answer, His leading, and His direction. We stay on a path of health and prosperity when we are led by the Spirit of God.

Remember to thank God for healing you!

FRIDAY

Ponder the path of thy feet, and let all thy ways be established. Turn not to the right hand nor to the left: remove thy foot from evil.
Proverbs 4:26-27

We are to be careful how we live and where we go. If we are to keep the Word in the midst of our hearts, we cannot be distracted by carnal influences. Once we are healed by God's word, if we are to stay healed then we must be careful where we go, and to allow God to establish our steps. What does it mean to have our steps established? When we get married, we establish our relationship with our spouses by our vows, and our commitment to them. We settle into a routine that we refer to as married life. This includes establishing a daily routine of coming home, greeting our spouses and children after they come along, acting affectionately toward our families and allowing love to prevail. We establish our ways by our routine, habitual ways of doing things. When we have made obeying God a routine habit, then our ways become established in Him. When we keep doing things this way, we keep our feet from taking us in the wrong direction. We can choose life and health and make it a lifestyle. We develop health by developing the habit of obeying God, following His word by giving it honor, first place and hiding it in our hearts. There is a wealth of health in God's word.

Remember...
By Jesus' stripes
YOU ARE HEALED!

WEEK SIX

Healing Scripture to Meditate for the Week...

If you are in need of healing, there is good news! Proverbs 4:20-22 SAYS:

"My son, attend to my words; incline thine ear unto my sayings. Let them not depart from thine eyes; keep them in the midst of thine heart. For they are life unto those that find them, and health to all their flesh."

So there is life and health in God's word. Since God's word is medicine, we must take it like we would a prescription. I suggest three times a day, like you would your food. Remember, healing is the children's bread. Consider this your "dose" for today. Remember, read, and meditate three times a day the following:

Rx: <u>Hebrews 13:8</u> ~ *Jesus Christ the same yesterday, and today, and forevermore.*

AND JESUS HEALED THEM ALL

MONDAY

And He came down with them, and stood in the plain, and the company of his disciples, and a great multitude of people out of all Judaea and Jerusalem, and from the sea coast of Tyre and Sidon, which came to hear Him, and to be healed of their diseases;
Luke 6:17

They came to hear and be healed. It is good to come to a Jesus meeting with expectation. Expectation is an essential part of faith. Without faith it is impossible to please God and to receive His blessings. With faith we can do many things. Faith can do the impossible. Faith can move mountains. Is there a mountain facing you in your life today? Then come and hear and be healed. Come with the purpose of hearing and being healed. This is God's way. Faith comes by hearing, and hearing by the Word of God. God blesses us tremendously when we hear His word. It is a blessing to us to hear the Word of God. He tells us to not harden our hearts when we hear His voice. If we keep our hearts softened then the Word becomes planted in good soil. This type of soil produces exactly what we hear.

If we hear words of healing, then we will believe that Jesus wants us well, and we will receive our healing. If we hear words of repentance, we will know that God expects us to live a life of holiness and will turn away from our wicked ways. If we hear words of prosperity, then we will know that meditating on the Word, observing and doing it, will cause us to have good success in all that we undertake. When we hear and believe God's word, we are healed.

TUESDAY

And they that were vexed with unclean spirits: and they were healed. And the whole multitude sought to touch Him: for there went virtue out of Him, and healed them all.
Luke 6:18-19

Are you vexed with unclean spirits? Spirits that torment and harass us will leave us when we come to hear and be healed. Jesus came to destroy the works of the devil. He went about doing good and healing all that were oppressed of the devil because God was with Him. He lived on earth as a man who was full of God. He was full of God's power and God's love. He says we can do the same works and greater works than He did. We simply need to be filled with God's power and God's love.

The love of God has healing and delivering power. Many people are healed and delivered from the power of unclean spirits when they hear the story of God's great love for us. When we hear the story about Jesus coming to earth as a baby, the growing up to defeat the devil and foil his plans for humanity, then loving and healing them all, then shedding his blood and dying in our place, we are moved with His love and compassion, and desire to forsake our sins and live for Him.

Remember...
Jesus Healed them ALL!

WEDNESDAY

And the whole multitude sought to touch Him: for there went virtue out of Him, and healed them all.
Luke 6:19

Because the whole multitude sought to touch Him, virtue went out of Him. This is sometimes referred to as making a demand with your faith. Faith makes a demand on the promises of God. Jesus always represents all the promises of God. He represents the will of God. He represents the virtue of God because as the Son of God, He is heir to all things. All power is in His hands. So why not seek to touch Him? When we touch Jesus with our faith, there is a transfer of His virtue to us. As joint-heirs with Him, we are entitled to receive all the things that our covenant promises. This includes the right to be free from all forms of disease.

If the enemy has put sickness upon you, then you have a right to be healed by touching Jesus. Come close to Him and learn of Him by reading and hearing His word. Find good faith-filled healing teaching tapes that cause you to believe that impossible, incurable diseases will be healed in Jesus' name. Find encouraging scriptures that cause you to come closer to Jesus. The whole multitude was healed, so there is no limit to God's healing power. If He healed the multitude, then He will heal you.

Remember...
He has Loved YOU
with an Everlasting Love

THURSDAY

> *And He said unto them, What man shall there be among you, that shall have one sheep, and if it fall into a pit on the sabbath day, will he not lay hold on it, and lift it out? How much then is a man better than a sheep? Wherefore it is lawful to do well on the sabbath days. Then saith He to the man, Stretch forth thine hand. And he stretched it forth; and it was restored whole, like as the other.*
> Matthew 12:11-13

Jesus likens His love for us to that of a man for his sheep. Then He declares that a man is better than many sheep. He declares that it is lawful for a man to be healed on the Sabbath Day. This was considered a day when no man was allowed to work, but Jesus said that if a man can rescue a fallen sheep from a pit on the Sabbath, then God will rescue us, fallen sheep from sickness on the Sabbath. This is good news. This means that we can expect to be healed at any time. There is no set date or time that God has chosen to heal us; it is merely a matter of our believing that Jesus healed them all. All includes you and me.

Are you waiting for God to heal you? Wait no longer! You are healed, since Jesus has satisfied the conditions for your healing. He suffered sickness so that you could go free. You cannot pay the debt twice. Even in natural law, to try a person twice for the same crime once He has been pardoned is considered double jeopardy and therefore illegal. Satan has to let you go once you believe that the penalty for your sins and sicknesses has been paid.

FRIDAY

> *Then the Pharisees went out, and held a council against Him, how they might destroy Him. But when Jesus knew it, He withdrew Himself from thence: and great multitudes followed Him, and He Healed them all;*
> *Matthew 12:14-15*

Are there obstacles to your healing? The Pharisees always protested Jesus ministry. There are Pharisees in our midst now. Perhaps it is some religious mindset that tells you that you must somehow earn your healing from God. Maybe it is fear. Perhaps it is relying on man, medicine or natural remedies. Sometimes we live in condemnation and feel unworthy to receive from God. Jesus knows about the obstacles. Sometimes it may appear that He has withdrawn Himself from our situation. When we focus on the obstacles, we do not exercise our faith and the Healer will withdraw Himself. Jesus' power and anointing will not be in operation when we focus on obstacles, unbelief, or fear.

But He is still our healer and He still healed them all. He is merely drawing us into a different path so that we will follow Him and focus totally upon Him. When our full focus is on Jesus, then we find our faith restored, our expectation increased, and our health begins to spring forth speedily. Here we see the multitudes follow Him again, and of course He healed them all.

Remember...
He will Never Leave you nor forsake you!

WEEK SEVEN

Healing Scripture to Meditate for the Week...

If you are in need of healing, there is good news!
Proverbs 4:20-22 SAYS:

"My son, attend to my words; incline thine ear unto my sayings. Let them not depart from thine eyes; keep them in the midst of thine heart. For they are life unto those that find them, and health to all their flesh."

So there is life and health in God's word. Since God's word is medicine, we must take it like we would a prescription. I suggest three times a day, like you would your food. Remember, healing is the children's bread. Consider this your "dose" for today. Remember, read, and meditate three times a day the following:

Rx: 3 John 2 ~ Beloved, I wish above all things that you may prosper and be in health even as your souls prosper.

THE MIRACLE CURE

MONDAY

Now Naaman, captain of the host of the king of Syria, was a great man with his master, and honourable, because by him the Lord had given deliverance unto Syria: he was also a mighty man in valour, but he was a leper. And the Syrians had gone out by companies, and had brought away captive out of the land of Israel a little maid; and she waited on Naaman's wife. And she said unto her mistress, Would God my lord were with the prophet that is in Samaria! for he would recover him of his leprosy. And one went in, and told his lord, saying, Thus and thus said the maid that is of the land of Israel.
2 Kings 5:1-4

Have you ever wondered why some people get healed and others don't? If you wonder about these things in the right manner, God will begin to bring answers to your questions. Perhaps this teaching will help some of you who have such questions. When I study miracles, I always like to look at the key persons and what they do in a miracle situation. In every miracle, there are certain elements present. Faith in God's healing power is the key element, and obedience to that faith on the part of the sick person is the other key element. The healing power of God works in His realm, the realm of the spirit and in heavenly places. How does one ascend into God's realm and receive a miracle?

Naaman the leper had been used by God to bring deliverance to Syria. The Syrians were not God's called-out people like Israel, but they received God's deliverance and obviously had God's favor and attention. Naaman used his talents to help God's cause. Be careful when you allow God to use you. You may be in line for a miracle. Naaman's wife's maid was a daughter of Israel. Just because there are Christians in your circle, it does not mean God will give you a miracle through them, but this little girl was a believing Israelite. There lies the difference. This little girl believed in the healing power of God that worked through the prophet. She was a prophetic person, because she walked through the house proclaiming God's healing power, if Naaman could just get to the man of God. She declared it so loud and with such faith, that she apparently got someone else to believe it and tell Naaman. Faith for a miracle has entered the atmosphere.

TUESDAY

And the king of Syria said, Go to, go, and I will send a letter unto the king of Israel. And he departed, and took with him ten talents of silver, and six thousand pieces of gold, and ten changes of raiment. And he brought the letter to the king of Israel, saying, Now when this letter is come unto thee, behold, I have therewith sent Naaman my servant to thee, that thou mayest recover him of his leprosy. 2 Kings 5:5-6

This little girl's faith was so strong that her words reached the ears of the King of Syria. Not bad for a little servant girl. Actually, this girl was a slave. She had been brought captive to work in the master's house. This is the way it is sometimes with people of faith. They may find themselves in unusual places because their faith is needed there. Even though circumstances are not favorable, God will elevate them if they use their faith to show mercy and compassion to others. Since faith works by love, this little slave girl apparently had a forgiving heart and was not resentful of her captors. Could you do that? Even in the workplace we sometimes have adversarial relationships with bosses and co-workers. Jealousy and competition cause us to view that fellow human being as more of an enemy than a friend. We have to determine to walk in love if we are to play a part in God's miracles. So love, the essential ingredient in all of God's work, was present in this girl's heart toward her master. This caused her words to have faith, to be heard, and to be carried to the highest authority in Syria. Will your words stand before Kings and Presidents?

Remember...
　　Give the Word Your Full
　　　　Attention

WEDNESDAY

And it came to pass, when the king of Israel had read the letter, that he rent his clothes, and said, Am I God, to kill and to make alive, that this man doth send unto me to recover a man of his leprosy? wherefore consider, I pray you, and see how he seeketh a quarrel against me. And it was so, when Elisha the man of God had heard that the king of Israel had rent his clothes, that he sent to the king, saying, Wherefore hast thou rent thy clothes? let him come now to me, and he shall know that there is a prophet in Israel.
2 Kings 5:7-8

Sometimes people are looking for a miracle from the wrong source. Many believers make this mistake. They assume that because they are a member of a certain church, that they can get all their needs met there. Maybe that is not your hang-up. Perhaps you are bound by your denomination. It makes no difference: bondage is bondage. Jesus warns us not to become entangled again with a yoke of bondage once we are set free. If you are looking for God to work miracles in your comfort zone, I'm here to warn you... He probably won't do it. Since God is the source of your miracle, you must go to one who ministers under the miracle working power of God. I hope your church does, but if not, ask God to lead you to the person who can get you healed. He knows who His servants are.

The King of Syria, while intervening for Naaman, writes a letter to the King of Israel requesting him to heal Naaman, even though the servant girl has told them to go to the prophet. Do different ministry gifts have different abilities? Of course, they do. Ministers differ by virtue of office, and whether or not they pay the price and gain the knowledge to minister healing. Some ministers could no more get you healed than that King could cure Naaman. At least the King of Israel had the good sense to let them know that he wasn't the one for the job. Many times we pray for people and have no faith, or sometimes even tell people that God perhaps does not want to heal them. It is not wise to assume abilities in God. We must know we have power, or we may give people a false sense of security or condemn them to remain in their infirmity. After some delay, the message finally gets to the man of God, who wants Naaman to know God's power. Is your miracle delayed? Keep pressing and hang on to faith. God will come for your faith. The delay may be testing your faith to determine the strength of it. It takes strong, persevering faith to get a miracle.

THURSDAY

So Naaman came with his horses and with his chariot, and stood at the door of the house of Elisha. And Elisha sent a messenger unto him, saying, Go and wash in Jordan seven times, and thy flesh shall come again to thee, and thou shalt be clean.
2 Kings 5:9-10

So Naaman is in the right atmosphere for his miracle. This is the other key element. We've seen the power of the preached or prophetic word to stir the heart of the recipient to put his faith in God. We've seen the tactic of the enemy: assumption that the one we choose will bring our miracle to us. Now we see the person with the power reveal himself to the receiver. What else is necessary? We will soon see that the attitude of the recipient is the last factor that must be aligned correctly in order for a miracle to be received. Elisha the prophet sends his messenger out with the Word of faith that will heal Naaman. Will Naaman believe and obey the servant's words?

The bible says that God sends His word and heals us, and that attending to the Word is medicine to us. Naaman, however, is unaware of this. He is looking for some type of honor from the prophet, when he really needs to humble himself and obey the Words that he hears. He has already delayed his healing by going to the wrong source. Going to the correct source always requires humility. Many sicknesses are a result of our pride. Pride causes us to sometimes neglect our health, destroy our health, or it causes us to neglect to incline our ears to the Word in order to be healed. Humility is the last factor to be dealt with here.

FRIDAY

But Naaman was wroth, and went away, and said, Behold, I thought, He will surely come out to me, and stand, and call on the name of the Lord his God, and strike his hand over the place, and recover the leper. Are not Abana and Pharpar, rivers of Damascus, better than all the waters of Israel? may I not wash in them, and be clean? So he turned and went away in a rage. And his servants came near, and spake unto him, and said, My father, if the prophet had bid thee do some great thing, wouldest thou not have done it? how much rather then, when he saith to thee, Wash, and be clean? Then went he down, and dipped himself seven times in Jordan, according to the saying of the man of God: and his flesh came again like unto the flesh of a little child, and he was clean.
2 Kings 5:11-14

Naaman was angry at the instruction of God. An angry spirit keeps the atmosphere around us tense and the Spirit of God is unable to penetrate that resistance until we repent. Sometimes we may feel anger if we have to wait for our healing, or if illness has stolen our ability to pursue what we desire. Naaman was angry because the healing was not going according to military protocol. He seemed to have a preconceived idea about how he was going to be ministered to and it wasn't working his way. Sound familiar? We want miracles, but we resent what we have to do to get one. Is your life not going your way? You may be on the path to your miracle.

The bible says a soft answer turns away wrath. When you are angry, God will send someone to you to give you a soft answer so that you can accept God's conditions for your healing. Naaman's anger was most likely the result of ignorance. Maybe he had been in charge so long that it was hard for him to admit his ignorance and submit to one higher in God's realm than he. God still holds us accountable to obey knowledge once it is given to us. Because of the entreaty of his servants, Naaman's heart was turned, he obeyed the Words of the prophet's servant, and he was healed. So the last element of the miracle was provided: the humble recipient obeys the servant whom God chooses to carry His word. Please take His word like medicine. It is life and health to all your flesh.

Titles by Rev. Barbara Williams:

QTY		PRICE	TOTAL
	God Wants Us to Be PROPHETIC PEOPLE (Vol. 1)	9.99	
	God Wants Us to Be PROPHETIC PEOPLE (Vol. 2)	9.99	
	THE MINISTRY OF THE WATCHMAN: Beacon of The Body of Christ, Keeper of The Lord's Lighthouse	11.99	
	7 WEEKS TO HEALTH AND HEALING (Vol. 1)	8.99	
	7 WEEKS WITH THE GOD OF ALL COMFORT (Vol. 1)	8.99	
	7 WEEKS WITH JESUS (Vol. 1)	8.99	
	PROVERBS WISDOM FOR WOMEN Prayer Devotional	5.99	
	PROVERBS WISDOM FOR MEN Prayer Devotional	5.99	

Prayer Manuals:

	"MINISTRY OF THE WATCHMAN MASTER PRAYER MANUAL: Prayers that Avail Much More; Making Known to Principalities & Powers the Manifold Wisdom of God"	19.99	

To order books, receive information about the Ministry of the Watchman, or to begin receiving The Ministry of the Watchman's annual publication, **The Lord's Lighthouse**,

Contact us:

1-800-560-9240

The Ministry of the Watchman International
P.O. Box 43334, Cleveland, OH 44143
office@ministryofthewatchman.com

For ministry itinerary, prophecies, testimonies, teachings and much more, visit us on the web at:

www.ministryofthewatchman.com

www.ingramcontent.com/pod-product-compliance
Lightning Source LLC
Chambersburg PA
CBHW061302040426
42444CB00010B/2472